BUSINESS ANALYST

JOB INTERVIEW

QUESTIONS & ANSWERS

Table of Contents

Introduction

The focal point of this book is to provide all the content and knowledge-base for individuals who are preparing to launch themselves as Business Analysts and have an interview scheduled for which they need to put their best foot forward.

This book is a product of Reelav Patel and Kriti Rathi's years of experience, who themselves are established professionals in the area of Business Analysis & Project Management. The authors of this book have poured down all their intellect and knowledge to help individuals who are either starting-off as Business Analysts or aspire to take their success stories, a notch higher.

The book brings forward all the Business Analysis questions that are commonly heard of and are highly expected in interviews. It does not include any domain-specific questions. This version of the book contains:

1) Business Analysis Questions
2) Situation/Scenario-Based Questions
3) Skills-Based Questions, and
4) Interview Tips
5) First Few Days as a Business Analyst

This book provides plentiful questions and answers, which, we hope may prove useful in your interview preparation. An analyst/job seeker can practice these questions prior to their interview and can be assured to come across as a confident, competent, and well-composed professional. Aside from sample questions and answers, the book also provides helpful tips to make the concepts easy to understand and some 'shine on' pointers for readers to stand-out in their interviews.

This book, in no accounts, is a short-cut to success; instead is an endeavor to equip all potential jobseekers and recognized professionals with the tips and tools of the trade so that they can build their careers based on a strong fundamental knowledge base.

This book is for you IF;

- You are determined to transform your career into the world of analysis and motivated to market yourself as a seasoned Business Analyst professional.

- You come for growth and are from different walks of professional life and have essayed different roles such as Developer/ Designer/ Quality Assurance/ Support Admin/ Project Lead/ Project Manager/ Business Advisor/ Consultant/ Process Engineer/ Administrative Engineer/ HR/ Project Co-Ordinator/ Non-IT roles, etc.

- You are already working as an Analyst and preparing for an interview for a better and improved role as a Business Analyst.

- You are a recent graduate or working towards completing a degree and are looking for a breakthrough as a Jr. Business Analyst/Business Analyst to jumpstart your professional career.

- You are a part of an organization's recruitment team and eyeing for a list of comprehensive and relevant BA interview questions & answers to familiarize yourself with this career line, help form an improved understanding of 'what to expect' from prospective applicants.

- You are specifically looking for plausible skills and situation-based questions and sample answers to hone your interview speech with.

This book is NOT for you IF;

- You are looking for detailed theory-based content on Business Analysis knowledge areas, or Business Analysis fundamental techniques.

- You are looking for a domain-specific interview guide, or You are looking for subject knowledge in the area where you analyze an organization (business) from various perspectives such as financials, market, growth, etc.

What you will learn:

- Simple, fun and easy ways to answer Business Analysis interview questions.

- Complete scripted answers to prepare for an interview.

- Techniques shared by the way of providing 'sample written answers' on how to blend content full of facts and personal experience in an impressive verbal manner.

- Smart ways to remember and answer questions by referring to answer tips.

- Situations, interview tips, skills-based questions and much more.

About the Authors

Reelav Patel, with over ten years of experience in Business Analysis & Project Management area, stands as a renowned professional in the Business Analysis industry. He has trained, mentored, and inspired over 2,000 individual Business Analyst professionals in the USA, Canada, and India. Over the years, he has transitioned as a successful entrepreneur, providing consulting and career development services to both young and experienced individuals, aiming to reach new horizons.

Kriti Rathi started her career as a Business Analyst for a private-sector organization, where she championed many successful project implementations in CRM and COTS builds. For the past seven years, she has progressed through many corporate ladders and is currently working for the provincial government (Ontario, Canada). Apart from her work commitments, she thoroughly enjoys mentoring and sharing her corporate wisdom with young minds on various public platforms.

Business Analysis Questions

1. How would you describe yourself?

OR

Briefly introduce yourself, elaborating on your experience & qualifications.

🎯 Discuss your experience, education, and credentials/certifications to answer this question conclusively. Focus on summarizing your experience as a Business Analyst in various domains, projects, methodologies, tools & techniques, and documentation; mention important responsibilities.

Need to stand out?

Gain extra credit by matching your key skills to the job requirements, you are being interviewed for.

Sample Answer: I

I have been working as a Business Analyst for the last five years. While working with well-known organizations such as *XYZ1* and *XYZ2*, I have strengthened my knowledge in Finance, Banking, Insurance, and Investment domains. As a Business Analyst, I have comprehensive experience in requirements gathering and analysis, creating context and technical documents, project management techniques, and testing & deployment areas of the project.

My recent project was with ABC1 Company as a Business Analyst. The project aimed at integrating and customizing the CRM system. I was responsible for designing, analyzing, and writing all the specifications and business requirements for this project. I was also responsible for managing back-end system design as well as piloting other sub-modules of the project.

My key responsibilities included conducting meetings and JAD sessions with the stakeholders and analyzing and documenting requirements in terms of solution. I was involved in creating BRDs, wireframes, UML diagrams, test cases, and UAT plans as part of the document deliverables. I used different business and software applications such as MS Word, Excel, Visio, SharePoint, Access, and SQL. I was involved in all the major phases of the system development, right from initiation till deployment.

I graduated from ABC University with a master's degree in Business Administration (MBA). I am an active member of the IIBA community.

ⓒ The following answer describes how a junior or non-experienced Business Analyst can answer the same question. You can discuss Business Analysis related responsibilities and skills you have performed in your previous job and co-relate the same as per the job requirements.

I have over two years of experience as a Software Developer in implementing, configuring, and supporting business systems in multiple functional areas of the organization.

I have closely worked with Business Analysts, Project Managers, and Quality Analysts throughout my current role. I have experience in business requirements elicitation & analysis and technical documentation, user acceptance testing, and managing change requests as part of the post-go-live support.

At the same time, I have extensive experience in creating solutions to complex business problems through process analysis & design, process re-engineering, and process automation.

I have experience in conducting and facilitating workshops and sessions with SMEs for product integration, upgrades and enhancements, and continuous improvement initiatives using Lean SIX Sigma, BPMN, and UML toolkit.

I have an in-depth understanding of the complete SDLC (Software Development Life Cycle), and end-to-end project delivery processes in various environments, including waterfall, agile, and scrum.

I graduated from ABC University with a bachelor's degree in Computer Science. Additionally, I have pursued CCBA certification from IIBA.

2. What are the problems solved by a Business Analyst?

🎯 This question can be answered in multiple ways. Various perspectives and problem areas can be discussed. Focus more on addressing high-level business problems and discuss potential solution as a Business Analyst.

Sample Answer:

A Business Analyst is a bridge between the client and the IT team. Business Analyst solves multiple business and stakeholders' problems, starting from requirements identification, analysis, design, and implementation.

Business Analyst solves the business/clients' problems and defines solutions in terms of requirements and provides functional solutions to the IT team.

Business Analyst is also responsible for managing change requirements throughout the project lifestyle. Business Analyst is responsible for creating scenarios & narratives and derives various business strategies and processes for the successful project implementation.

Business Analyst micromanages the project

13

deliverables and manages the team, which eventually leads to project success.

3. How do the responsibilities of a Business Analyst differ from a Project Manager?

Sample Answer:

Usually, a Project Manager is the one who attends to questions/matters relating to the 'project,' whereas, a Business Analyst is someone who focuses on the 'product,' aka solution. In certain organizations, there may be an overlap between the duties of a Business Analyst and Project Manager. However, organizations do need both the roles to maintain a clear distinction between their activities.

Generally, A Project Manager defines project milestones, deliverables, and timeline; outlines scope; creates acceptance and rejection criteria; builds resource allocation charts; while a Business Analyst is responsible for managing stakeholders and requirements as well as micro-managing the project for successful delivery.

A Project Manager develops project plan and scope documents, whereas Business Analyst develops requirement documents, BPMN, BRD, use cases, test cases, and UAT plan.

A Project Manager prepares stakeholder engagement

14

and communication plan; in contrast, Business Analyst performs stakeholder analysis, defines techniques, including RACI and P to I (Power to Interest) matrices, and collaborates with stakeholders to finalize requirements.

There are times when a Business Analyst is expected to perform the typical duties of a Project Manager. It is a Business Analyst's core responsibility to understand the granularity associated with the business' needs and propose solutions capable of solving associated issues. Moreover, Business Analyst facilitates requirements sessions, passes on reasoned, and final requirements to the development team.

4. What was your role and responsibilities in the recent project?

Ⓖ Discuss the project highlights, major responsibilities and project deliverables, adding achievements and/or project success related to the project is a plus.

Sample Answer:

My most recent project involved customization and software enhancement, aimed at improving the back-end system of a financial institution. I was responsible for defining the scope, requirements elicitation, analyzing needs and solutions, devising strategies, facilitating stakeholder collaboration, and ensuring milestones are achieved as per the defined timelines.

The purpose of the project was to enhance and streamline back-end processes. As a Business Analyst, I was liable to ensure that business stakeholders understood the requirements and necessary functionalities were built to support stakeholder's engagement with the system. With the project's successful implementation, we were able to provide a consolidated and flexible back-end system, which met the initial needs of our clients.

I was also in charge of ensuring change requirements were duly captured, reviewed, and approved by the management. The careful analysis was done to ensure new requirements did not lead to scope creep. I performed UAT and reported bugs for issue tracking.

5. **Do you have experience in Project Management? What project management tools have you used?**

Business Analyst may not have direct experience as a Project Manager, but generally, a Business Analyst reports/works closely with a Project Manager. This, in turn, provides significant insights about the duties performed and tasks undertaken by a Project Manager.

Need to stand out?
Provide more info on any Project Management tools that you have used, such as MS Project, JIRA, Clarity, Confluence, or Advanced Level Excel skills.

Sample Answer:

As an experienced analyst, I've practiced and sharpened my interpersonal, communication, and behavioral skills to work with project team members and external stakeholders. My profession has allowed me to collaborate with Senior Management and recognize the principles of project management to practice successful team-leading techniques. This has led me to hone my timeline management, resource & task allocation, and budget management skills.

In the last (X) years, I've used a range of project management tools such as MS Project, Jira, Success Factor, and Workday. Exposure to such tools has allowed me to manage projects successfully.

6. **What are the different documents a Business Analyst prepares?**

Business Analyst prepares a wide variety of documents throughout a project lifecycle, depending on the methodology followed/

practiced by an organization. In a traditional (Waterfall) environment, a Business Analyst is responsible for the creation of Business Requirements Document (BRD); however, in an Agile environment, the focus is on the formation of user stories.

Sample Answer:

Over the years, working as a Business Analyst, I have prepared various documents including Requirements Management Plan, BRD (Business Requirements Document), SRS (System Requirements Specification), User stories, UAT plan, Training manuals and UML (Unified Modeling Language) diagrams such as Use Case, Data Flow, Activity, Sequence and Entity-Relationship.

Business Analyst also assists the Project Manager in preparing the project plan and project scope documents. An experienced Business Analyst contributes till the testing phase by developing a test plan and test case documents along with Quality Analyst.

Business Analyst plays a vital role in a project team by producing additional documents such as Scope of Work (SOW), Request for Proposal (RFP), and Business Case, which are imperative documents for project delivery.

7. Explain SDLC.

OR

Explain the SDLC and role of a Business Analyst in each phase.

⊚ This is a fundamental interview question and is not frequently asked in the interviews; still, you need to understand the basics of the complete SDLC cycle to be able to successfully answer this and other similar questions in a methodological manner. The question is geared at you 'selling' why someone in a project management domain should hire you. Convince the interviewer how you as a Business Analyst, add unique value at every step of the way, and that your skills are transferable across lines of business, and varying methodologies adopted by the organization.

You can cut and trim the answer below according to your needs as it is written fundamentally and covers all phases in detail.

Sample Answer:

Software Development Life Cycle (SDLC) is the most commonly followed process in any software project. It entails a thorough blueprint establishing in what ways to create, sustain, or improve a specific software or its components. It specifies an approach for developing the software by categorizing which tasks should be performed when and allows for monitoring of the overall development process. It is used in nearly all project management environments (mainly by IT analysts) when building or reengineering software systems.

Initiation & Planning

During this phase, high-level planning and scoping meetings amongst executives and project sponsors occur. These are done to obtain a clear understanding of what the project team will be set out to build.

As vision and scope discussions take place, a Business Analyst is required to ensure that the project undertaking churns up collaboration across the organization, and different stakeholders participate in the planned scope of work activities.

Typically, the Business Analyst assumes the role of a facilitator during this time. They assist the project sponsor by including relevant users in discussions, forming agenda items, forecasting risks or challenges with meeting logistics, etc.

Requirements Gathering and Analysis

During this phase, a Business Analyst works with business owners and stakeholders to elicit requirements that the solution must fulfill. It is the 'requirements analysis' phase with which SDLC truly takes the centerstage.

Business Analysts are expected to not only elicit requirements but to also manage them by prioritizing them against importance/risk, sorting them against type (business vs. stakeholder vs. solution vs. transition), and constantly update those requirements. Requirements are also depicted by creating use case scenarios, user stories, or wireframes that illustrate different functionalities/ features desired in the software solution under different conditions.

It is imperative that a Business Analyst obtains appropriate signoffs on the documented requirements as they are then considered comprehensive and complete.

Design & Development

After the requirements are finalized, design workshops are initiated by system analysts/architects to code the software solution systematically. Experienced Business Analysts with technical familiarity also contribute meaningfully along with system analysts during this phase.

A Business Analyst supports a Systems Analyst by meeting stakeholders to finalize technical decisions imperative for implementation. A Business Analyst may also facilitate design workshops by bringing together the business and technical teams and having them flesh out design specifics.

During the development phase, software developers often work closely with the Business Analyst. This is done to ensure developers have a full grasp of the business requirements they are expected to code. Business Analysts can provide the context related to many of the listed requirements, which eases out developers' work during unit testing and reduces code errors.

Testing

After development, the prototype/code goes through different rounds of testing. Generally, there is an internal testing to check if the code works as expected and then system testing to ensure that the software solution works as per requirements when interfaced with other systems.

During testing, the Business Analyst provides the User Acceptance criteria and work closely with testers to make sure that the criteria are met. Business Analysts also cross-check the initial requirements with the working solution and create a log of deficiencies.

Deployment & Support

During the deployment phase, the solution is implemented and is made available to relevant stakeholders for use.

Based on its operationalization, the business users may come up with 'new or revised' enhancements (change requirements), which also get managed by a Business Analyst, like how they did during the Requirements Analysis phase. Depending on the project's scope and timeline, new iterations could also form, which may lead to a new SDLC to commence and similar duties being repeated by a Business Analyst.

8. What is the difference between BRD, SRS, and FRD?

Start the answer by demonstrating your knowledge of these documents and explain in a few sentences what these documents are about, before discussing their differences. Depending on your business domain and processes and standards followed by your organization you may have noticed that some prefer one over the other. The easiest way to do any theoretical explanation is by linking your content with how you have used it in your experience. Discuss which of these documents you have worked on previously and if you follow any structure (format). While answering, try to be as close to the fundamental answer as in the sample below and, if asked for clarification, explain how a Business Analyst can make necessary adjustments to any of these documents to meet the organization's requirements criteria.

A Business Requirements Document (BRD) intended to provide high-level business and stakeholder requirements is generally created by a BA during the initiation phase of a project, whereas a Software (system) Requirement Specifications (SRS) is intended to provide a detailed log of functional and non-functional requirements accompanied with use cases and can be developed by either a BA or a BSA. An SRS document is usually worked upon during the planning phase.

A Functional Requirement Specifications (FRS), alternatively called Functional Requirements Document (FRD), is created to comprehensively provide functional requirements to the reader. It is often accompanied with UML diagrams, including data flow and activity. Usually, an implementation lead, developer, or a BA is seen working on these documents.

A BRD can be prepared even when a BA may only have access to high-level project requirements; however, an SRS or an FRD can only be prepared when low-level (detailed) solution requirements have been fleshed out.

As a BRD contains information on the business's background, needs, existing requirements, and attempts to answer the 'why' a project or its requirements have been undertaken, its main review audience is middle and senior management. These decision-makers are predominantly concerned with understanding the true need of a project; hence, the document is kept at a high-level.

An SRS generally attempts to answer 'what' requirements should be fulfilled to achieve project goals; while an FRD attends to the 'how' those requirements are expected to function. These documents are system focused; hence, its audience generally is PMs, tech leads or SMEs.

In my previous role, I was assigned to create a BRD for a COTS project that my organization had undertaken. I ensured it covered enough context for an executive reader to grasp the content easily as well as be specific enough for use by the project team, including developers during the design and development phases. I also took responsibility to maintain a version history with the document so that all major changes and updates to the business requirements can be captured in an organized way.

9. **Explain UML and your experience in developing Use Cases?**

    Discuss your experience in developing one or

more of UML diagrams, which includes: Use Case, Data Flow, Activity, Sequence, Entity Relationship diagram, etc. Pay emphasis on known UML types and focus on Use Cases when discussing UMLs. These diagrams can be created using any UML creator/software, but the most recognized tool is MS Visio. Make sure to practice Use Cases before the interview, so you are better prepared to develop if asked.

Sample Answer:

The Unified Modeling Language (UML) is a graphical representation of a system. It is a standard language for stipulating, visualizing, building, and detailing the artifacts of a software/system. The UML signifies the collection of best engineering practices that have proved to be successful in the modeling of vast and intricate systems. Various known types of UML diagrams are Use Cases, Data Flow, Activity, Sequence, and Entity-Relationship.

I have extensive experience in developing Use Cases. I created use cases to document the procedural flow of an actor's interaction with the system. Use Cases define system boundaries or high-level scope of a project and describe various functionalities by illustrating possible scenarios a system offers. Each scenario can be decomposed into the use case script(s), which mainly includes primary flow (main/standard/normal/happy flow), alternate flow, and exception flow.

10. Make a Use Case Scenario for an ATM.

It is imperative to understand and demonstrate the users' expectations in use case modeling. A perfect use case scenario/diagram should depict and be able to achieve what the user wants in their interaction with the final system. It is equally important to keep your use case diagram succinct by avoiding long names/elaborative descriptions in a use case and by employing 'noun + verb' rule. Actors in a use case model should not be personalized to an individual's interaction with the system; instead, it should be role-based. Actor notation in a use case diagram must be used to define any specific role's interaction with the system and not the individual person's interaction. Below is a description/summary of commonly used Use Case Diagram notations.

Symbol	Description
	Actor: A user that interacts with the system.
	System: A system component that can contain multiple use cases. This represents the system's boundary.
	Use Case: A unit of functionality provided by a system.
_____	**Association:** Associates actor or system with the use cases.
– – -<<include>>– –> – – -<<extend>>– –>	**Dependencies (Include, Extend):** Shows dependent use cases as an extension to the primary use cases. **Include:** This dependency indicates the use of one-use case (secondary use case) in conjunction with another use case (primary use case) to complete a functionality. **Extend:** This dependency

	indicates the use of one-use case (secondary use case) in conjunction with another use case (primary use case) to add an additional functionality.

Sample Answer:

ATM Machine Use Case Diagram

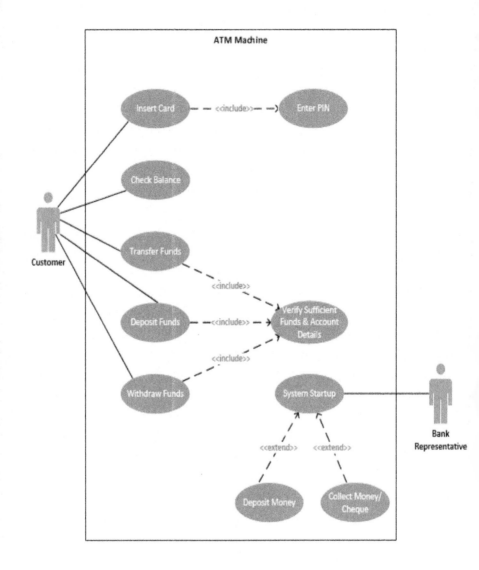

11. Write a Use Case script for cash withdrawal from the ATM machine.

⊚   Each use case scenario in a use case diagram can be decomposed into the use case script(s). Use case scripts should be written in a step-by-step manner, aiming to define one use case scenario from start to finish. Each script should contain elements as defined in the example below, focusing on three different flows; primary flow (main, standard, general, or a happy path), alternative flow, and an exception flow.

It is recommended not to include human errors outside the domain of a system while discussing alternate and exception flows.

Sample Answer:

Use Case ID: UC0001

Use Case Title: Withdraw cash from ATM machine.

Date Created: MM/DD/YYYY

Use Case Description: This use case describes how a customer uses an ATM machine to withdraw cash from his bank account.

Actor(s):   Primary: Customer
        Secondary: Bank Representative

System(s):   ATM

Trigger/ Pre-requisite/
Related Use Cases: UC0005, UC0007

Pre-condition(s):   The bank customer must possess a valid ATM card.

31

Post-condition(s):	1. ATM returns the card and dispenses cash to the customer. 2. ATM registers the transaction to the customer's bank account.
Normal Flow:	**S01:** Customer inserts an ATM card **S02:** ATM machine requests the PIN no. **S03:** The Customer enters the PIN no. **S04:** ATM authenticates the PIN no. **S05:** Customer selects account type from available accounts (Chequing or Savings) **S06:** Customer selects 'Withdraw' from the available menu options **S07:** Customer selects/enters the withdrawal amount **S08:** Customer confirms the amount **S09:** Machine ejects ATM card **S10:** Customer collects dispensed cash **S11:** ATM offers an option to Print Receipt **S12:** Use Case ends (exit)
Alternate Flow:	**A01 @ S03: Customer enters wrong PIN no.:**

1. The system prompts the customer to re-enter the PIN
2. Customer re-enters the PIN
3. Resume @S04

A02 @ S06: Customer enters an invalid amount
1. The system displays an error message "Invalid amount entered. Please enter a valid amount."
2. Resume @S07

Exception Flow: **E01 @ S03: Customer enters the wrong PIN no. for more than three consecutive times:**
1. The system prompts a message "You have exceeded the maximum number of allowed attempts for PIN verification. Please contact your bank."
2. Use Case ends.

12. Explain Agile.

Sample Answer:

Agile is an iterative, collaborative, and incremental approach/methodology/framework/process of software development. The agile methodology assumes rapid collaboration between cross-functional teams, promotes adaptive planning, is iterative in execution, and focuses on quality-driven solutions through continuous improvement. In an Agile approach, product or process can be divided into small incremental builds/phases/iterations; each iteration generally lasting approximately 3-8 weeks; with every iteration involving cross-functional teams working simultaneously on various areas, such as; planning, requirements analysis, design, coding, unit testing, and acceptance testing.

Agile methodology promotes customer collaboration and rapid change request handling throughout the software lifecycle.

13. Define Scrum (OR Agile-Scrum).

Sample Answer:

Scrum is a subset of Agile. It is a lightweight framework and the most widely used Agile methodology. A Scrum process is distinguished from Agile processes by specific concepts, practices, and methods. Scrum environments typically allot three key roles: A Scrum Master, Scrum Team, and Product/Project Owner. A Business Analyst may play the role of a Scrum Master or can be a part of the Scrum Team, depending on the project.

The features/requirements to be developed are

categorized as the product backlog. A complete product backlog can be divided into small sprint backlogs, and each sprint may range from 2-4 weeks. The features/requirements are described as **user stories**.

There are four different types of meetings that are typical in an Agile-Scrum environment:

i. Sprint Planning: This is the first meeting that is held at the beginning of a new sprint and typically lasts up to 2 hours. This is a very critical meeting where the scope of work is determined by planning and reviewing sprint backlog items.

ii. Daily Stand-up: This is the foremost meeting that occurs every day and lasts for up to 15 minutes. This is when the Scrum team gathers to discuss their work; each team member shares their minutes regarding what they did yesterday. What the plan to do today and/or follow up reports on any special assignments or obstacles hindering their progress.

iii. Sprint Review: At the end of the sprint, the Scrum team holds the sprint review meeting to discuss accomplished goals/milestones throughout the sprint. This meeting usually lasts for an hour but can be extended depending on the length of the sprint.

iv. Sprint Retrospective: This is the last meeting,

held after the completion of the sprint. This meeting gives an opportunity to the sprint team to review developed functionalities and derives lessons learned to be applied to future sprints.

14. Explain product and sprint backlog in a Scrum environment.

The product backlog is generally a term used to define the number of requirements in an Agile-Scrum environment. This is usually managed by a Product Owner/Project Team. A Business Analyst is expected to pull many hats in an Agile-Scrum environment; he/she could also be the one who manages the product backlog in the capacity of a Product Owner.

Sample Answer:

The product backlog defines the requirements for the project. These requirements are generally written in the form of user stories, prioritized by the highest customer value. It is managed by the product owner, updated, and refined over the project cycle as information and requirements are gathered.

At the beginning of each sprint, the team reviews the product backlog and identifies the high-priority user stories which are to be completed within the sprint timeline.

There are two types of Scrum backlogs:

i. Product Backlog: The total number of user stories to be developed for the entire project is called "product backlog." This is created once and maintained over the life of the project. The product backlog is usually updated/reviewed on a *weekly* basis.

ii. Sprint Backlog: The number of user stories to be completed in one sprint is called "sprint backlog." This is created at the beginning of each sprint; it is managed by the project team and contains a detailed list of all the tasks that the team must complete for each user story in the sprint. The Sprint Backlog is updated/reviewed daily.

15. What are the different types of Scrum meetings?

Sample Answer:

There are five different types of scrum meetings.

i. Sprint Planning: These meetings are held at the beginning of a sprint, where complete sprint activities are planned. Usually, all team members, including Scrum Master, Product Owner, and Project Team are the participants. In this meeting, the team discusses the major product Backlog items and estimates the delivery for implementation.

ii. Daily Stand-Up: This is the first meeting of the day, scheduled every day, at the same time, with the same group. In this meeting, all project team members gather and discuss their major activities/involvements from the previous day, as well as their actions/ meetings/plans for the current day. Although not a common occurrence, any changes to objectives, milestones, or new obstacles found are discussed so that the entire team is aware.

iii. Product Backlog Refinement/Backlog Grooming: This meeting is primarily aimed at addressing any changes or grooming of existing Backlog items. Here, the approach is to discuss and finalize any modifications required to the existing functionalities in the Backlog.

iv. Sprint Review: This meeting is held at the end of a sprint, where discussions around deliverables and functionalities that were structured during the sprint cycle take place.

v. Lessons Learned/Sprint Retrospectives: The team discusses the sprint's successes and defines 'lessons learned' to avoid future failures.

16. What are User Stories?

⊚ It is fairly common for beginner Business Analysts to mix up User Stories with Use Cases and Test Cases. All these are distinct terms with specific meanings. User Stories are used in an Agile-Scrum environment. Use cases are a type of UML diagrams, which can also be written as Use Case Scripts to describe requirements. Test Cases are procedural flow for testing system functionalities, written by a Quality Assurance Analyst.

Sample Answer:

A User Story is used in an Agile-Scrum environment to capture and describe a set of requirements. These are written, keeping end-users'/stakeholders' perspectives in mind. User stories should be written in a way that makes it understandable by both the development team and business users. A user story can be written on flashcards, which induces brainstorming activities within the stakeholders' group.

User stories should be prioritized according to the highest value they render to the stakeholders, paving a roadmap to product development. Each project may have several user stories which are categorized as a product backlog. The product backlog can be broken into small, multiple sprints, and stories to be developed in one sprint are called sprint backlog. Each sprint is usually 15 days long. Normally, a project team develops 30 user stories (approximately) per sprint.

The recommended format to write a user story contains the below components:

Who: This term describes a role/persona/user.
What: This term describes the requirement or a function or action.
Why: This term describes the value of implementing the user story.

17. Explain the role of a Business Analyst in different methodologies?

Although the primary role of a Business Analyst does not change in different methodologies, the responsibilities may vary as per the method the organization is following. The Business Analyst's role differs mainly in the areas of documentation, client collaboration, team administration, and requirements management.

Sample Answer:

The primary role of a Business Analyst does not change between different software development methodologies, although the tools and techniques used by a Business Analyst can fluctuate according to the needs and aspects of any given project or development lifecycle.

Business Analyst's role in the predictive

environment (Waterfall) is substantial in gathering, analyzing and documenting requirements into a BRD, whereas, in an adaptive approach (Agile), they would be more inclined towards facilitating conversations with stakeholders and developing user stories.

In a predictive approach, the Business Analyst connects with the stakeholders in the initiation, planning, and requirements phase of the lifecycle and does not respond to the changes until deployment. However, in an adaptive environment, the Business Analyst collaborates with the customers throughout the lifecycle, hence, responding to the change requirements at all phases of the lifecycle.

Business Analysts typically work individually and independently in a predictive environment. On the contrary, undertaking various roles and working in cross-functional teams is a crucial element in an adaptive environment. It is expected of a Business Analyst to operate in a prescribed manner in Waterfall as the duties are responsibilities are pre-defined, while in Agile, the role is evolutionary and pushes for innovation.

18. Discuss JAD (Joint Application Development/ Design).

Sample Answer:

JAD stands for 'Joint Application Development/Design.'

JAD is a requirement-design and software development methodology in which stakeholders, subject matter experts (SME), end-users, software architects, and the project team attend meetings to outline a system's high-level scope/requirements. JAD focuses on business problems rather than technical details. Harmonized group synergy, effective leadership, and the excellent coordination skills of the facilitator are all catalysts to a successful JAD session.

The purpose of JAD is to bring together IT and the business community in a structured workshop setting in order to extract high-level system scope/requirements.

JAD sessions are usually conducted during the initiation phase of the project. However, they can be held on a regular basis.

The key participants in a JAD include the Executive Sponsor, Project Manager, Business Analyst, Stakeholders, Scribe, and Development Team. Generally, JAD sessions are led by a Project Manager, accompanied by a Business Analyst, although, a Business Analyst can also facilitate JAD sessions on an on-going basis.

JAD leverages group dynamics, extensive use of visual aids, documentation, prototypes, and an organized process designed to gather and define requirements in a short timeframe. JAD reduces the amount of time needed to gather requirements, shortening the overall development duration.

19. What is a business case, and what is your experience in creating one?

(◎) Mention having professional experience with creating business cases. Typically, a business case includes vital information related to the project, such as an executive summary, reasons (for undertaking a project), associated cost, timeline, risks, forecasted revenue/benefits, business options, and investment appraisal.

Sample Answer:

A business case is a proposal document created by the project team to convince decision-makers or project sponsors to approve a project and/or funding.

A well-crafted business case explores all feasible approaches to a given problem and allows business owners to select the option that aptly attends to the organization's needs.

An ideal business case offers strategic solutions and benefits for the proposed problems; it contains the problem statement, objective, proposed solutions, analysis (SWOT, Market, PEST, Risk, GAP, Cost-Benefit, Financial Projections, ROI – Return on Investment, etc.), timeline & milestones, project management plan, recommendation, and conclusion.

I am proficient in creating a business case document, both for a new project or change management initiatives. In my last role, I was a part of the project team that created a Business Case document during our project initiation phase. I was the lead Business Analyst, responsible for conducting the market and financial analysis for the business case document.

20. What is your experience in business process analysis?

Business process analysis is one of the core perspectives of Business Analysis. To conduct business process analysis effectively, it is imperative that a Business Analyst has a sufficient understanding of the current and future state of the project. BPMN and Activity Diagrams are the most commonly used tools to perform effective Business Process Analysis.

Sample Answer:

Business process analysis is an imperative step towards the successful delivery of a project. It is performed for all types of projects, whether a project is aimed at system enhancement or system configuration or business process re-engineering. Business Process Analysis can be undertaken at any stage of the system development life cycle, but it is primarily executed during the initiation & planning stage, where the scope is analyzed, and desired functionalities are discussed. Project scoping and requirements documents are also drafted and finalized for stakeholder reviews.

I have an all-embracing experience in business process analysis & management. In my most recent job, I conducted business process analysis using BPMN (Business Process Modeling & Notations) and designed various process flows. Based on these process flows, I performed a GAP Analysis to understand the current state ('As Is') of the system and created future processes ('To Be').

I followed a systematic framework while conducting the business process analysis, which included the following steps:

Step 1:
Careful analysis performed to design 'As Is' and 'To Be' process flows and analyzed pre-requisites, inter-dependencies, and outputs.

Step 2:
Used UML tools such as MS Visio to create process models.

Step 3:

Continually implement changes in order to optimize the desired business processes.

21. Explain any two requirements gathering techniques?

🎯 You can explain any requirements gathering techniques, such as interviewing, brainstorming, questionnaires & surveys, scenario building, task/document analysis, JAD sessions, use cases, focus groups, prototyping, observation sessions, etc. Discuss any of these techniques used in your previous experience as a Business Analyst/related role.

Sample Answer:

In my experience, multiple requirements gathering techniques can be used in a single workshop/session to gather requirements from stakeholders. I would like to explain Interviews and Brainstorming techniques.

i. Interviews are the most common approach used to gather requirements. This technique establishes a one-on-one relationship between the facilitator (Business Analyst) and the stakeholder(s). Interviews can be structured or unstructured. Structured interviews are the ones where a Business Analyst prepares questions *prior* to the meeting. In an unstructured interview session, questions are formed *spontaneously*, based on the meeting discussions. Both techniques can be used simultaneously or separately in a session. Before conducting interview sessions, I prepare the meeting agenda, questions/topics for discussion, and a checklist of tasks. I strategize my questions to be both open-ended and close-ended.

ii. Brainstorming is another excellent requirement(s) gathering technique, which promotes innovative thinking for a given problem. In my last job, I conducted several brainstorming sessions with a focus on extracting as many stakeholders' views and opinions as possible on any given requirement or scenario. In this approach, I aim to acquire a comprehensive understanding of a requirement by encouraging stakeholders to provide a pool of ideas rather than limiting their ideas. This technique helps to gather multiple ideas, which can later be evaluated according to their importance in the project and can be further distributed to the stakeholders.

22. Explain BRD (Business Requirements Document).

Sample Answer:

BRD is a 'Business Requirements Document.' A Business Analyst prepares this document based on the

47

requirements gathered and analyzed from stakeholders. A Business Analyst may use different techniques to gather requirements such as brainstorming, interviews, JAD sessions, use cases, scenario building, task analysis, and focus groups. Based on the Business Analyst's interaction with the stakeholders, he/she prepares a BRD, which contains business requirements, functional & non-functional requirements, system, and user-specific requirements.

I have extensive experience in writing BRD. A typical basic structure of a BRD comprises of:

Introduction:

This section includes objective, project scope, project background, document approach, business drivers, existing systems, risks, business assumptions, and acronyms & abbreviations.

Business Requirements:

Generally, this set of requirements includes business needs, policies, guidelines and/or day-to-day business operations. In essence, this section provides insights into the business objectives and outcomes.

UML & Process Flows:

This section mainly contains UML or BPMN diagrams to derive high and low-level business and functional requirements.

Functional Requirements:

This section discusses how the system operates/behaves based on a specific input. Functional requirements can be illustrated using use case diagrams and can be further decomposed in terms of use case scripts.

Non-Functional Requirements:

Non-functional requirements cover multiple criteria, such as adaptability, availability, certification and compliance, compatibility, extensibility, maintainability, manageability, performance, portability, privacy, reliability, security, scalability, usability, which the system must meet in order to operate efficiently.

Appendix:

Any additional/reference data, screenshots, or related information is included in this section.

23. What is your experience in conducting UAT?

Sample Answer:

I have remarkable experience in preparing and conducting UAT sessions with stakeholders. Typically, UAT sessions are conducted with users prior to system deployment.

In my recent project, we deployed system releases every three months, and I conducted UAT session(s) before each release.

In preparation for UAT sessions, I prepare a UAT plan document, which mainly covers project deliverables, change requirements management plan, test cases, and test data. Once prepared, I share this document with the stakeholders *prior* to the meeting and schedule a kick-off meeting, when/if required.

While in a UAT session, I provide a system walk-through and encourage stakeholders to perform testing by executing major test cases. I generally offer relevant test data and training manuals to support testing. The ultimate objective of this activity is to get the approval of stakeholders on the UAT. Change requests derived from the session are analyzed carefully with the project team, and I conduct follow-up sessions to resolve these issues with the stakeholders.

24. Explain the defect lifecycle?

Discuss different defect statuses and defect management activities, along with defect tracking tools. The widely known tools are HPQC/ALM, JIRA, Bugzilla, and IBM Rational ClearQuest. Also, discuss any automation testing tools you have used; known automation tools are Quick

Test Professional (QTP), Selenium, Load Runner, etc.

Sample Answer:

Defect management is a vital phase of the Software Testing Lifecycle (STLC). As a Business Analyst, I have been an integral part of the testing process in most of my projects.

Defect/Bug lifecycle generally comprises of different statuses of a bug/defect. When an error is found, the status is set to 'New'; as soon as the defect is reported to a developer, the status changes to 'Assigned'; after being assigned, developers can choose to 'Accept,' 'Reject' or put the defect in a 'Deferred' status. If the defect is accepted, status changes to 'Open' or 'In Progress.' Sometimes, defects can be deemed "non-actionable" due to various project constraints; and developers can then choose to set the status to 'Rejected' or 'Cancelled.' Sometimes, a 'Deferred' status could mean canceled, but this is usually logged with a valid reason (i.e., it may still be a defect but is determined to be not feasible to resolve in the current iteration).

Once developers resolve the defect, the status changes to 'Fixed.' Most bug-tracking tools like Bugzilla, JIRA, or ALM will notify the testers about the updated status (i.e., bug resolution) and will create an action for them to 'Re-Test.' While re-testing, if the testers find a defect, yet again, they will reassign the same defect, and its status will be set to 'Reassigned.' After another fix by the developers and following a testing round by the testers, the final status will be set to 'Closed.'

25. What is your experience in risk management?

Risk management is a core project management area usually directed by a Project Manager. As a Business Analyst, we are primarily involved in managing requirements risk and dealing with on-going project risk. A Business Analyst can manage and control requirements risk by developing a requirements management plan and/or risk registry.

Sample Answer:

Risk management is one of the most important aspects of Business Analysis. It is one of the core responsibilities that a Business Analyst is expected to perform throughout the project lifecycle. Overhanging requirements, hybrid approach to software development, scope creep, or vague requirements can all lead to requirements risk. A Business Analyst handles such risks by maintaining a risk registry. A risk register includes a risk ID, risk details, consequences, impact, priority, probability, risk level, risk modification plan, and information of a risk owner.

I believe a competent Business Analyst performs risk analysis by identifying areas that may adversely affect the solution by understanding their impact, communicating consequences, and developing a risk mitigation plan for the management. It is recommended to communicate newer risks or statuses on existing risks to the stakeholders.

I have confidently and effectively demonstrated these best practices of risk management in *all* my previous projects. This approach has led me to deliver the projects successfully and manage risk components efficiently.

26. Explain stakeholder analysis. What techniques have you used to perform a stakeholder analysis?

Sample Answer:

Stakeholders are individuals who are a part of a project team with a vested interest in project development. The term 'stakeholder' generally refers to clients, users, customers, or SMEs.

Stakeholder Analysis technique defines 'how the stakeholders may impact solutions' or 'be impacted by them.' Business Analysts carry out a stakeholder analysis to determine stakeholders' interests, behavior, and level of involvement in a project. Stakeholder analysis can also be used to identify potential project risks in the early stages of project development.

I have used different types of Stakeholder Analysis techniques, including Stakeholder Matrix, RACI matrix, and Power to Interest ratio. RACI matrix is the most widely used stakeholder analysis technique, which correlates stakeholders' relationships with pre-defined project deliverables. The roles are defined as:

R – Responsible
A – Accountable
C – Consulted
I – Informed

A Power to Interest/Influence grid is another stakeholder analysis technique that classifies stakeholders' power and interest in a project. It is represented in four quadrants, and each quadrant denotes power versus interest ratio, e.g., High Power – High Interest, High Power – Low Interest, Low Power – High Interest, and Low Power – Low Interest. Each stakeholder's name/position is added to each quadrant as per their power and interest distribution in the organization.

Situation/Scenario-Based Questions

Situational interview questions provide an excellent way for an applicant to emphasize his/her past accomplishments and highlight outstanding professional skills and competencies. These questions also offer ample 'personality assessment criteria' for the Hiring Manager/Human Resources panel to make hiring decisions.

Not all questions in a job interview will be situational; however, an upward trend is being increasingly noticed with the number of such questions being asked (consider at least 1/4th of interview questions). It is recommended that you sketch high-level situations related to the few topics below (and more!) before the interview day and practice your speech. Unlike other typical 'content-oriented' or 'technical' questions, these should sound less like a rehearsed speech (don't be too artificial) but should not make you go blank (or spell-bound). If you have a few situations crafted/thought-through from previous experiences in your head, chances are you can readily employ those situations and swiftly navigate through such questions. Your answers should emphasize that you focus on issues and facts as opposed to people's or your own opinions.

A genius came up with a STAR acronym for answering these questions:

S – Situation:
What is the context (background/ scenario) of your situation?

T – Task:

What impact did the situation have on your tasks? How does the situation affect you?

A – Action:

What is it that you did? How did you resolve the issue? What strategies/skills did you employ?

R – Result:

What was the outcome of your actions? Did you learn something new about yourself? Learned new people/task management skill? How does this improve you today? How can you bring this new strength to the table for the job at hand?

We like to think of these questions as 'story-narrations' with a recount of positive learning for you. We recommend not to overemphasize 'What Happened?', instead, emphasize 'What did you do?', all in no more than three minutes. Often, candidates focus more on following the exact STAR pattern to answer such questions, which should not be the case. If you cover the high-level problem in a situation and its resolution, you are on the right track.

1. How do you resolve stakeholders' conflicts?

OR

What if the stakeholders do not agree with each other's solution or have an internal conflict? How would you manage such a scenario?

Situations or conflicts may arise due to different reasons. Sometimes various stakeholders may have varying understandings of a single component of a system, or simply put, some requirements are complex in nature. No matter what the situation is, exceptional coping and coordination skills can mitigate any conflicting scenarios. Discuss having experience in resolving stakeholder conflicts. It is not always that you will have the exact same situation experienced from before; in that case, you can talk about any related or similar situation from the past.

Sample Answer:

I would like to talk about my recent project, where I had to deal with the conflicting views of stakeholders during a requirement(s) gathering workshop. Our workshop intended to finalize the requirements related to the various roles associated with the staff management module of the project. Subject Matter Experts and technical stakeholders had dissenting views of the domain and project functionalities. The domain group challenged the technical group's understanding, and their request was to accommodate ten generic roles in order to manage various hierarchies in the organization. Furthermore, these roles were not defined by the domain group, which led the technical team to question the implementation of such incomplete information.

I used my analytical and problem-solving skills to evaluate the entire situation and decided to gather information separately from both groups temporarily. This approach allowed me to focus on both groups' rationale for differing recommendations/requirements.

Using my proficient technical skills, I created wireframes to demonstrate the system design. Based on further discussions with the groups, I suggested four master roles - one for an Advisor, Supervisor, Manager, and an Additional role for contingency access. This additional role met the domain group's need for having the flexibility to create multiple roles within the system as required.

Both groups accepted this solution, and we were able to proceed with only well-refined requirements. This solution allowed the technical team to easily incorporate it with the back-end system design.

By channeling effective stakeholder management and communication skills, I was able to identify the right business requirements, resolve conflict, and create an amicable work environment.

From all my past experiences, I can conclude that conflicts are inevitable in any project, but it is their thoughtful management that can harmonize relationships without risking the *timely* implementation of solutions.

2. **Do you have experience in managing stakeholders who may change requirements frequently?**

Respond to this question in affirmation by developing a story (STAR technique of answering). The intent of this question is for the interviewer to figure out whether you can manage a project with the presence of 'various stakeholders with various needs.' Express yourself in a way that reinstates that you have 'people' as well as 'business' skills. Talk about the importance of staying on track with the project timeline and how you have achieved that by following a systematic strategy when challenged by stakeholders with uncertain requirements.

Sample Answer:

In my last project, I worked with a team of advisors, most of who joined the project mid-way through the Requirements Gathering phase. As such, they did not possess the same understanding of the project as others who were on board from the inception.

As quite predicted, I had the struggle of bringing them on the same page as everyone else when running requirements workshops like focus groups and interviews. Often, I was given a set of requirements by the stakeholders, which were either already implemented or deemed out of scope.

When this started affecting the project timelines and deliverables, I had to rejig my requirements elicitation approach. I began to kick-off my meetings by going over the project scope document with the stakeholders and reiterate the objective that we were set to achieve. This provided a conscious undertone to our activities as well as set the direction for requirements elicitation. I also employed a reverse-engineering technique, which at its core, endeavored to link back all the requirements to the primary objective of the project. Although this approach worked the majority of the time, yet in certain situations where the requirements did not match the stakeholders' expectations, I created paper prototypes/system mock-ups to create possible scenarios that eventually eliminated redundant/vague requirements.

I also have vast experience with Change Management/ Change Control Process in various methodologies. In situations where stakeholders made modifications to requirements 'too soon', a formal, written-out change order form was expected to be filled out by them. I thoroughly assessed change orders to ensure new/revised requirements did not lead to scope creep or budget/resource issues. A review committee was set up to analyze the impact of those changes on the project's cost and timeline. All these measures ensured requirements did not just 'wishfully' change, but in fact, were vetted through a formal and coordinated process.

3. **Describe a time when you introduced a new idea or process to a project and how it improved the situation?**

This question is centered on knowing your interpersonal and decisive analytical/leadership skills more than knowing which organization/ position you were in at the time you suggested a new idea. This question can be answered in multiple ways. You can either discuss a novel approach you took to something that was stagnated/inefficient/outdated, either in the work sphere or from personal experience. The question is aimed at knowing if you harbor innovation/creativity and can be a self-starter. Your answer should convey that you can identify an issue that needs improvement and act on it immediately to bring in heightened efficiencies.

While working at XYZ, I was the lead BA on a COTS project implementation. As under any Business Process Management Perspective, the first and foremost issue at hand is to standardize and streamline many 'similarly aimed' processes into something which reduces un-advantageous dependencies and further refines the processes.

I started the project by inheriting many such redundant and time-consuming processes. As it had been a few years since any business process reengineering endeavored in the organization, I initiated discussions with key internal partners and drew people's attention to features that required updates.

I formed a mid-size team of 8 participants and created a GAP analysis document. I geared the review approach on items that had the most impact on COTS software implementation and gradually worked my way through areas that had less impact on it.

Regular process review meetings offered members a chance to brainstorm ideas designed at improving current processes and developing new processes that had clear lines of reporting, communication, and task assignment. By clearly defining roles & users and outlining associated tasks, it gave way to eliminate unnecessary requirements.

A pilot launch of the new initiative was undertaken for a six-month period, and adjustments were made to fine-tune on-going review & monitoring activities. I am confident to say that the organization truly benefitted from my approach, and this was credited to be one of the significant reasons for the success of the project.

4. **Describe a time/situation when you worked under a high-stress environment. How did you handle the high work-pressure and your workload?**

This question is asked because the hiring manager is interested in knowing how you can manage piled-up work. It is typical for certain positions (like Project Coordinator, Business Analyst) that you would be required to take on tasks that have not been done in a long time (such as backlog items). Your answer should directly clue the employer into thinking that your organization skills are an excellent match for the position. It is also recommended to not 'pass on the blame' to others in your team, as it may look bad on you as a team player. Talk about the 'situational-reasons' for the overload and not 'personal.'

Sample Answer:

I would like to discuss a situation when my previous

company had successfully acquired a new business, and we were required to shift the new client-base to our existing database in a short period of time. These activities needed to wrap up around the same time as the implementation month of the project I was already working on. As a Business Analyst, I was expected to handle my 1st project and supply new project's requirements to the technical team within the defined timeline.

I, along with the support of my Manager, planned for the work ahead of us and created a work-breakdown structure for both the projects. For the existing project, I delegated some of the responsibilities to my colleague Business Analyst and took upon more of an oversight role under my Project Manager's awareness. I shortened the frequency of my touch-point meetings with the project team to every three days from *weekly* so that there is a fast turn-around, quick decision-making, and early identification of matters requiring escalation. For my new project, I worked closely with the Project Manager, SMEs, and Database Architect on a regular basis. I assisted the Database Architect by developing Entity Relationship Diagrams to provide a technical relationship between the tables and data.

Careful planning and organization of tasks helped deliver both the projects within the allotted time. I learned how to effectively manage the project team and work as well as not let the high-stress environment affect my performance.

5. **You are contracted to gather requirements for a software implementation project involving multiple divisions of an organization. Each division is going to provide requirements, and there are roughly eight divisions. How will you go about gathering the requirements?**

The answer to this question should establish your experience and know-how of conducting different types of requirement gathering techniques. The employer wishes to learn how you would change your requirements gathering techniques when conducting sessions with small versus large groups, groups with similar versus distinct needs, and from experienced stakeholders to stakeholders who could be relatively new to the organization. In your answer, mention how you facilitate different requirement workshops by gathering, analyzing, finalizing, and documenting requirements that you are given from the workshop sessions.

Sample Answer:

In one of my projects, I served as a client Business Analyst for a solution provider company. For this project, I was required to gather requirements by working with several SMEs and analysts from multiple agencies - which were our clients and vendors.

I encountered challenges when big/large-sized agencies dictated the majority of the system requirements by virtue of their domination in the project. This was exerted by the high influence they had on the overall functioning of the solution when compared to agencies that were relatively smaller in sizes. Nevertheless, each agency had a significant role and input to provide in the finalization of the project, and I made sure not to compromise that equation.

Initially, I worked with the SMEs and analysts from various agencies and vendor companies directly in the meetings. As consultations progressed, I used to discuss/brainstorm the requirements with all participants and analyze the given requirements in the meeting itself. Due to limited system familiarity/ knowledge possessed by the SMEs, workshops started running over the scheduled times and it became apparent that not all SMEs participated in the meetings. As smaller agencies felt their input hardly got count in the meetings, they started to refrain from having active, engaging discussions. This in turn, temporarily resulted in moving at a slower pace than what we were required to.

To resolve the situation, I worked with the SMEs from each agency on a one-on-one basis. Prior to each meeting, I would create a presentation/deck by doing extensive document analysis (by researching the current artifacts) and gathered high-level requirements by holding virtual meetings with each agency separately through "GoToMeeting." This approach of 'document analysis' and employing some 'interviewing techniques' allowed for every agency's requirements to be heard and provided ample time so that I can analyze and shape those requirements in ways that attracted the highest consensus. Additionally, I provided those high-level requirements to agency analysts ahead of actual meetings, so they are just as prepared to navigate workshops in a direction that allowed for unanimous agreement.

Through my tact and judgment, I was quick to change gears on my requirements gathering style from JAD-like sessions to smaller, more personal, interview-style technique and finalized requirements without derailing the schedule from where recovery would have cost a fortune.

Skills-Based
Questions

1. What are your strengths?

🎯 Always discuss your Business Analysis expertise or related strengths. Strengths from other areas could be brought up as well, with greater emphasis to be given to highlight your forte in Business Analysis. Remember to prepare at least 2-3 strengths ahead of the interview. Generally, strengths do not require an explanation as compared to weaknesses.

Sample Answer I:

While working as a BA for X years, I have sharpened my analytical thinking and problem-solving skills, along with my competent Business Analyst skills.

Sample Answer II:

I have also developed project management skills, including time and resource management. This has allowed me to manage project deliverables even under tight timelines and limited resources.

Sample Answer III:

I thrive on new challenges and look for avenues to gain as much knowledge as I can. I thoroughly enjoy reading business articles and connecting with industry experts to gain from their insights.

Sample Answer IV:

I have postulated domain-specific expertise in the areas of banking, retail, and insurance, along with my technical skills.

2. What are your weaknesses?

You may choose to talk about your weaknesses from other or related business areas, but it is recommended not to bring forward vulnerabilities from the Business Analysis profession. It has been noted that employers/HRs do not appreciate 'disguised weaknesses' (attributes which truly are strengths, but one chooses to position them as weaknesses), such as:

- I am too good to be true, and I think my team members have an issue with that, so I am trying to counterbalance my skills.

- I like to make sure that I achieve surpassing perfection in my work; thus, many times, I find myself spending way extra time ensuring my work is error-free.

- When I am working on a project, I just don't want to meet deadlines. Rather, I prefer to complete the project well ahead of schedule.

- Being the perfectionist that I am, I do not just meet the deadlines; instead, I complete all my tasks way ahead of time as compared to my counterparts.

- These will be professional faux pas, so stay away from sugar-coated weaknesses!

Sample Answer I:

Sometimes, I spend more time than necessary on a single task or take on tasks personally that could easily be assigned to someone else. Although I strive not to miss a deadline, it is still an effort for me to know when to move on to the next task. To overcome this, I have started assigning priorities to my tasks and organize project deliverables accordingly.

Sample Answer II:

I struggle with delegating tasks to team members, due to trust and performance reason that they may not be able to accomplish the tasks within the given timeframe and with the same quality. To get rid of this weakness, I have started to define milestones and deliverables before handling work to anyone. This approach has hugely benefitted me and others in my team as trusting working-relationships are built.

Sample Answer III:

I have a great experience working on multiple tasks concurrently, but there are some tasks that require extensive research, analysis, and undivided attention. In order to deliver all wide-ranging tasks within the expected timeline, often, I have observed that quality gets compromised. To overcome such, I now ask for help early-on or request extensions so that those tasks requiring expertise and extra due-diligence, do not get compromised.

Sample Answer IV:

When responding to stakeholders' requests/requirements, I used to spend a lot of time discussing simple requirements, which had led to failure in accomplishing meeting agenda in a single workshop. I have learned to prepare for a solution before the session, to eliminate extended discussions over simple requirements.

3. How do you handle failure as a Business Analyst?

The way you answer this question could stand you out in terms of how you handle and resolve project or requirements failure. This question is disguised under two intentions:
I. How transparent are you in acknowledging your failures?
II. What have you learned, or what is your approach when you are struck by a failure?
You do not necessarily need to talk about

project failure, but if you choose to, common examples can be - not meeting the timeline, not meeting the client's exact expectation. Discuss your many skills such as organization, people, and task management skills, your proficiency in improving tasks and processes. You should sound honest and convincing at admitting your failure(s) while building the interviewer's confidence that with your capabilities (e.g., keeping sanity intact, focus, and positive attitude), you can overcome any project failure.

Sample Answer:

I consider even a small issue in the project/not meeting the client's requirement on time as a failure. I like to be professional and proactive in terms of my work commitments, regardless of the methodologies and processes being followed. This strategy allows me to stay on top of my tasks and strike a balance between project scope and timeline without getting failures affect my performance for long.

In my last project, we had missed the implementation date by two weeks, which was mainly attributed to unexpected personal issues faced by two of the key members in my team. I, being the lead Business Analyst, did not foresee that such a situation would have adverse consequences on the project delivery at the time.

As anyone going through a tough time may do, the performances of my team members started deteriorating. My mistake being, I failed to flag this situation to senior management early-on and not devising a mitigation plan. Nevertheless, as we missed the 1st schedule date, after that I was quick enough to realize where we had gone wrong and asked for additional resources. Looking back, I can say, re-defining scope and asking for timely help were my two biggest learnings. I take pride in knowing that a calm and composed head and determination to strike back on, with improved zeal, are my mantras to handle any failure and for it to not become a repeated activity.

4. Where do you see yourself in the next five years?
OR
What is your career plan?

If you are a Junior Business Analyst, focus your answer more on building Business Analysis skills. Saying something like, "I want to become a Project Manager, right away" may not be a great strategy. Say something like you envision becoming a Project Manager in the long run (after three years or so). Mentioning of quick/immediate transition does not show long term affection/ connectivity/ commitment to the Business Analyst job. If you are an intermediate/senior Business Analyst, then discuss how you want to avail experience in different domains, roles, and your commitment to achieve that. You can bring forward any certification you are preparing for or any efforts made to enhance your skills/education portfolio.

Sample Answer:

I've been practicing Business Analysis for the last two years, and I want to grow as a Senior Analyst and eventually a Project Lead. To attain those roles, I am sincerely expanding my domain know-how and learning the duties/responsibilities undertaken by a Project Lead.

I just pursued my Scrum Master Certification, and I am now preparing for CCBA certification. I have recently started an online course to brush-up my technical skills.

5. What are the skills required by a Business Analyst?

It is recommended to discuss the few skills listed in the first point below. In addition to that, you can (should) discuss other Business Analysis skills. Having stated positive skills does not require in-depth clarification. Simply stating them and/or elaborating in 1-2 sentences, is good enough.

Sample Answer:

The most important skills required by a Business Analyst are communication skills (verbal and written), interpersonal skills, domain and technical knowledge, behavioral characteristics, and analytical thinking and problem-solving skills.

I have learned and developed different other Business Analysis skills like documentation, organization, and management skills and team management. I like to stay abreast of new tools as I thrive on learning new technologies.

6. Why did you leave your last job?

It is not recommended to talk about personal situations at the interview time. (e.g., conflict with team/manager).

Sample Answer I:

My recent project is over.

Sample Answer II:

Due to the simple and repetitive nature of projects, there is no opportunity to grow in my current job, and I want to further pursue my career as a Senior Business Analyst by facing newer challenges and expand my skillset.

Sample Answer III:

I have worked at my current organization for the last four years and have honed my experience and skill set. I feel confident to take on more responsible roles that will steer me to think/act outside of my comfort zone.

My company is downsizing currently, although, I have not been notified of any decisions, I am proactive in my job search to secure a position in an established and continuously growing organization, like yours. My Project Manager is well-aware of the situation, and I will be able to provide excellent references, if and when required.

7. **Why are you a good fit for this job?**
   OR
   Why should we hire you?

You should match the job requirements, including education, certification, and experience, while discussing this question. If you can match the 'must-have skills' listed in the posting, it significantly improves your chances of landing the job offer. If you are pursuing something (educational courses, honing a skill), you should mention that as well. Extra points can be accumulated if you can convince the hiring manager of how you would be an asset to the company. In your answer, you should not sound too boastful/bragging about your experience, which may imply 'employer's loss' in not hiring you.

As your company is looking for a candidate with decent experience in using CRM tools, I have been designing, customizing, and implementing CRM applications for the last X years. In particular, I have been credited with a successful CRM application customization in my last job, whose domain is similar to yours.

This position's educational requirements also assert a preference over someone with a bachelor's degree. I earned my bachelor's in Computer Science and went on to completing master's from XYZ University with a special area of emphasis in Business Improvement and Technology.

As stated in the job requirement, you are looking for someone who is an expert in the documentation. I am confident to say that I consider myself an expert in creating Business Analysis documents, including BRDs, UML diagrams, user stories, UAT plan, and training manuals.

In addition to bringing superior communication and proficient documentation skills to the table, I bring along the fine art of building and maintaining client relationships. I have demonstrated this ability in my last role by leading vendor procurement and project implementation activities.

Interview Tips

- Dress professional and sharp. Go with tried and tested clothing ensembles:

  > **For men:** Dark color suit, a pair of dress shoes, a matching belt with shoe color.
  > **For women:** A suit or dress with a blazer can also be opted, depending on comfort.

- Pay attention to small details in your attire: tied buttons for shirt/sleeves, polished/clean shoes, neatly tucked-in shirt, spotless, and steamed clothing.

- Stay away from accessorizing your look too much (it may not look work-appropriate).

- Any visible nails (fingers/feet) should be properly trimmed, should look presentable.

- Breath should be odorless. Do not chew gum during the interview process. If you had chewed a gum right before the interview, rinse your mouth or drink some water not to smell strong.

- Do not spray strong fragrance cologne in excessive quantity.

- Well obvious but often missed: put your phone on silent mode or switch it off.

- If you are wearing a digital watch, make sure it is silent and does not make any notification sounds while you are in the interview.

- If you get stressed/tensed before an interview, do things that comfort you down (e.g., quick meditation). Talking to your friends, family, mentor right before an interview also boosts confidence. You should present yourself confidently and professionally.

- Greet the interviewer/panel with a firm handshake and appropriate greeting.

- Carry along three hard-copies (no fold, no wrinkles) of your resume and keep some samples of your work or work-accomplishments, in case you get asked to present.

- For the first five minutes, you will have the maximum attention from the interview panel, make sure you practice well the 'About Yourself' question.

- Clarify any interviewer's questions/concerns about your profile in detail if they have any.

- Practice the STAR (Situation, Task, Action, and Result) technique of answering situation-based questions. Provide examples from previous employment experience and fine-tune to bring forward an answer which resonates with your personal style and is believable.

- It is advisable to link your situation/story to some deficiency that you had witnessed while in the situation. You will have all buy-ins from the recruitment panel when you answer in a way that elaborates on 'how you make decisions.' This helps the hiring manager recognize your core decision-making mechanism, leadership skills, resourcefulness in accumulating information, and your ability to make sound decisions.

- Make sure your speech does not make you sound brash about your achievements and convey others as a failure. If you must talk about a negative incident, talk with humility and sincerity in your speech (it does not sound professional when you snitch about your co-workers, and portray yourself as the only righteous person).

- Learn all the skills, keywords, and abbreviations mentioned in your resume. It can really count against you if you are unable to explain anything from your resume.

- Do not interrupt the flow of the interview, by asking questions before you are given a chance to ask. The interviewer will give you enough time to ask questions that you may have prepared from before/thought about during or after the interview.

- This book takes a holistic approach to providing Business Analysis interview questions and answers. It is recommended to read through the sample questions and answers a couple of times. Prepare the first few interviews by practicing your answers in front of a mirror or friends and family.

- Pay attention to your facial expressions and body language throughout the interview. Maintain eye contact with all the panel members.

- Research the company and interviewers' profile. Also, prepare your answer, 'why do you want to work for this company?'

- Do some research well before the interview regarding the salary range for the experience you possess, the industry you would be interviewed for and the job requirements.

- Do not initiate salary/compensation discussion, unless initiated by the interviewer. Always have a desired salary range in mind for each position (e.g., $65,000-$75,000 annually). If it is a contractual position, provide an hourly rate range for the compensation expectation.

- Some sample questions that you can put forth for the interviewer (it is wise to prepare a few questions ahead of the interview):

o   Can you discuss more about the project?

o   What is the team-size for this particular project?

o   Methodologies of processes being followed

o   Further steps in the hiring process?

o   How is performance measured in this role?

- Send a 'Thank You' note on the same/next day of the interview, expressing your gratitude for taking the time to interview you. Show how you are still excited to be a part of the team. Make sure the note is short and sweet. You can follow-up with the hiring contact after a week or so.

- Any answer should not exceed two to three minutes. You may need to adjust the answer time, depending on the question. Do not speak too fast or too slow. Watch your pace, specifically when the interviewers are making notes of your answers.

- As the interview gets wrapped up, exit while thanking the panel with a solid handshake. Express how you await the decision.

- At last, it is not always necessary that you get selected for the position you interviewed for, even though your interview went well. Do not feel demotivated or lose hope if you fail the interview(s). Remember, it is a process, and it may take time and revisions. You should keep putting in efforts and hard work in the right direction and eventually, you will achieve success.

First Few Days as a Business Analyst

This section explains the day to day procedures of starting a new role; it also defines the key initiatives taken by a Business Analyst in the first few days. This daily routine may help you understand BA role even more clearly.

All information in this section is of high importance for a new or experienced BA. It is advisable for all "BAs" not to undermine this section. Find below the practical and real-time day to day process.

Day 1

- I arrived at the workplace as early as 15-20 minutes before my reporting time. I wore regular office attire and was not super dressed up as this was going to be a regular workday.

- Prior to my start, I had received an instructive e-mail from the HR manager, which detailed reporting time and who to contact along with some information on parking at the facility. I was also informed to bring some identification card cards and void cheques for the payroll set up.

- At 8:45, I checked-in at the reception and asked for the concerned person. At security, I was given a visitor's tag as a means of identification for the day, which I was expected to return by the end of the day.

- Approximately at 9 AM, I met with the HR Manager. After exchanging greetings, I was given a quick tour of the building and took that as an opportunity to introduce myself to the departmental personnel in IT, Marketing, and Project Management Office.

- After engaging in pleasantries with my new colleagues, there was an orientation program scheduled in one of the board rooms, for new hires, including myself.

- I was provided with an overview of the company's operations which included familiarization around its market position, customer base, accountability to reporting bodies and other functional aspects.

- The presentation was well put together and a valuable source of information as I learned many key things about the company I will be working for. The Director of the department I was going to work for did a brief stint in explaining what they do, their strategic clients, processes that they have in place, current active projects, and their existence in the specific business domain.

- Around noon, we had lunch, and I was accompanied by my PM and Director of applications.

- After lunch, I was shown a presentation on workplace safety, security, and insurance, which was later followed by a quick chat with the HR on the internal Code of Ethics & Policies & Procedures.

- Orientation was concluded by the IT dept. where they briefed us on company's IT tools, systems/softwares in use, and training on Intranet.

- I was provided with a work laptop and given a short walk-through on accessing relevant files and drives.

Day 2

- I submitted the required paperwork to the HR and also had my permanent access card handed over.

- With the help from the department's Administrative Assistant, I set up my desk phone, desktop screens and installed drivers for printing.

- (It is not necessary to know all the technical part about how to connect and get access to various devices in order to start up your work. The support team is always there to help you. Keep the support contact emails handy as you may come across some technical forest-up issues in the first few days.)

- Initially, I copied/CCed my immediate supervisor/ PM, on all communications initiated by me.

- I had to request the developers to grant me access to the tool I was assigned to work on. They provided me with the access and a quick walkthrough of the tool. The usability seemed a bit complex as this was my very first time using the particular tool, but with the help of training manuals, I picked up on the software after a few attempts/playing around.

- Later on, I attended a team meeting where project objectives, milestones, timelines, and my responsibilities were discussed

  (This project was more of an enhancement initiative, so I could benefit from the working application (up & running) to formulate my understanding about the system and rely on its configuration for my AS-IS requirements.)

- I was proactive in the session and asked several questions related to the application and project to get the facts and figures straight.

- It was agreed that I'd meet the PM for 30 mins on a daily basis for a few weeks to discuss many deliverables/tasks on the project. Concurrently, similar meetings were to be established with the development team so that I can further clarify my understanding of the technical aspects of the system.

- I was diligent in taking meeting minutes, identifying follow-up actions on my laptop, which later did in fact, help me prioritize the tasks, and stay on top of my commitments.

Day 3

- I checked my meetings for the day and responded to emails first thing in the morning. Later on, I continued to work on drafting the use case scripts and polishing the draft project plan, which I had created the previous day.

- (Usually, as a BA, you do not prepare the Project Plan as has been discussed earlier in the book; it is a part of the job function of a Project Manager. Here, I was also playing the role of a Project Lead, so this was one of my responsibilities.)

- A meeting was scheduled with developers today, and I was able to learn more about the existing tools; Mainly focused on learning about the domain and existing application.

- Towards the end of the day, I shared a status update document with my manager, which tracked the tasks assigned to me and their status to completion. I also forwarded working documents for their review.

Day 4

- I was asked by the PM to set up recurring meetings with the business advisors starting next week, and I did so by firstly checking the attendees' calendars and ensuring there were no/minimal conflicts. Secondly, I prepared a meeting agenda which basically included Application status, List of new requirements, open discussion topics, follow-up questions, notes, and remarks).

- I also spent time updating the RACI matrix, which I had started preparing the previous day.

- In addition to that, I spent my afternoon working on updating process flows and creating new use case scripts with a team member.

- Working with a team member allowed me to understand the writing style that goes in this organization (as some may have their own way of writing use case scripts) and only record correct/valid details.

- Gradually, I started obtaining positive feedback from my team/PM on the work I have been doing in the last few days. This boosted my confidence and inspired me to continue working smart in the achievement of project goals.

Day 5

- Finally, one of my major requirements documents got approved by users, although some of those requirements were later modified as user participation/attendance increased in my meetings (this document consisted of 4 requirements in total).

- I continued working on previously undertaken tasks and updating documents.

  (By day 5, work seems to be getting simpler as my familiarity rises).

- In a meeting today, I discussed the next steps in the development plan with the technical team members.

- For the next few days, I will be working to finalize, gather, and document new requirements with the stakeholders. Upon completing this, I intended to share the document with the developers, and concurrently work with the business and technical teams to deliver the project modules.

Key Takeaways

The first few days as a "BA" in any domain may seem overwhelming because you are processing a lot of information, also trying to understand and retain most of the aspects of the project. This gets much easier later on once you acquire all the knowledge required and start utilizing it efficiently. The more you understand the nuances of the project, the easier it becomes eventually. Use your Business Analysis skills by taking notes and analyzing different documentations to make the whole process fun.

- If you are a consultant and work on various projects/jobs, you will get acquainted with the process, and it will become natural after the completion of the first job.

- It is advisable not to get too excited in the beginning by amassing all the responsibilities and later stressing yourself out to deliver on those tasks. Your efforts should concentrate on understanding the details, facts, 'As-Is' scenarios at best in the first few days and raising questions along the way as things get confusing. Don't make assumptions. Ask, Ask, Ask!!!

- Initially, obtaining clarity on the project is crucial than trying to narrow down the low-level requirements. In other words, if the bigger picture of the project is unclear/tainted, you may not get the requirements right later on.

- Brush up your knowledge on everyday tools. You always have to have a decent hold on basic applications as there likely be selected training for them and asking too many/inappropriate questions about their usage is not very professional. Rather watch some online videos or read about them and polish your familiarity. It's okay to ask questions when you have tried to help yourself but did not succeed. Do the homework first, and later ask for help.

- Try to divide/organize your queries/questions by departmental heads.

- Technical questions should be directed to the technical team members such as developers and designers

- Project-related questions, such as those on deliverables, timeline and objectives can be asked to the project manager

- Requirements related questions should be

clarified with users or stakeholders. Initially you will not be connected with the business stakeholders, in those occasions clarify with the Sr. BA or PM or the concerned person you report to For the initial few weeks/months, try to prepare documents for all the work you do Preparing a meeting agenda and sharing it with your attendees ahead of the meeting is a great habit. There are many recommended 'in-built' templates with increasingly all software which you can use with, when unsure of how to approach something new.

That would be it BAs...

Hope you had a wonderful time reading this guide, we wish you the absolute best success as a Business Analyst!

Other Related Books You May Like:

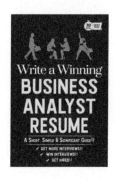

WRITE A WINNING

BUSINESS ANALYST

RESUME

Find us on Amazon @

www.amazon.com/dp/B07X6PYS5X

PROJECT MANAGEMENT

JOB INTERVIEW

QUESTIONS & ANSWERS

Find us on Amazon @

www.amazon.com/dp/B07YVP4MCX

Notes

Notes

Printed in Great Britain
by Amazon

58882370R00061